Published by Addax Publishing Group, Inc.
Copyright © 1999 by Steve Cameron
Designed by Randy Breeden
Cover Art and Illustrations by Brad Kirkland
Cover Designed by Laura Bolter

All rights reserved. No part of this book may be reproduced or transmitted in any form or by any means, electronic or mechanical, including photocopying, recording, or by any information storage and retrieval system, without the written permission of the Publisher.
For Information address:
Addax Publishing Group, Inc.
8643 Hauser Drive, Suite 235, Lenexa, KS 66215

ISBN: 1-886110-73-5

Distributed to the trade by Andrews McMeel Publishing
4520 Main Street
Kansas City, MO 64111

Printed in the USA

1 3 5 7 9 10 8 6 4 2

Library of Congress Cataloging-in-Publication Data

Cameron, Steve
    101 ways to enjoy baseball : appreciating the finer points of our national pastime / by Steve Cameron ; illustrations by Brad Kirkland.
     p. cm.
    ISBN 1-886110-73-5 (hc.)
    1. Baseball—United States—Humor. I. Title. II. Title: One hundred one ways to enjoy baseball III. Title: One hundred and one ways to enjoy baseball
GV873 .C26 1999
796.357'0973—dc21

99-21239
CIP

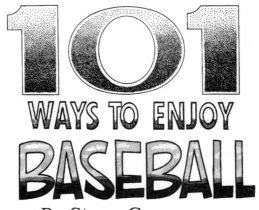

101 WAYS TO ENJOY BASEBALL

By Steve Cameron

Illustrations by Brad Kirkland

DEDICATION

For my dad, who taught me how to keep score.

TABLE OF CONTENTS

Acknowledgements 7

Introduction - The Game 9

Baseball for Kids 19

Baseball for Women 47

Baseball for the Expert 83

DEDICATION

For my dad, who taught me how to keep score.

ACKNOWLEDGEMENTS

Nobody does a book alone, even a fun little project like this one.

Thanks, first of all, to everyone who loves baseball and has passed some of that enchantment on to me.

All my appreciation, once again, to the folks at Addax Publishing Group — especially Bob Snodgrass and Darcie Kidson — for putting me to work.

(If you can call this kind of enjoyment work...)

Our book would be nothing but a string of silly words without the drawings of Brad Kirkland, who can make you smile at almost anything.

And finally, another deep bow to wife, Sylvia, not only for her support but some first-rate editing.

She even likes baseball. How great is that?

INTRODUCTION

THE GAME

Everyone knows Abner Doubleday invented baseball.

Unless it was Alexander Cartwright.

Or maybe someone else.

In any event, America's national pastime most certainly has its historical roots firmly set in the tiny village of Cooperstown, N.Y.

Although perhaps it originally was played in England. Come to think of it, partisans of the game don't totally agree on anything — except that artificial turf is the work of the devil and that you should never end an inning being thrown out at third base.

Oh, one more thing unites the boys and girls of summer.

Almost to a person, they hate football and smile at the words penned by conservative columnist and dugout junkie George Will: "Football combines America's two worst traits — violence punctuated by committee meetings."

Baseball fans are serene (critics would say smug) in the knowledge that theirs is the one true athletic pursuit. They revel in its poetry and understated passion. They point to the game's rich history, even to its amazing body of literature. A true aficionado can discuss the hit-and-run play as though nuances of that particular strategy may have been revealed in the Dead Sea Scrolls.

Want to kill a few hours?

Walk up to any group of serious bleacher bums and ask sweetly: "So why would Dennis Eckersley throw Kirk Gibson a breaking ball in the '88 World Series?"

Wars have started over lesser disputes.

True fans, by the way, will tell you that baseball itself has achieved such purity that it is beyond the gripes of any particular generation.

No other sport, they'll argue, remains immune to better training, bigger and faster athletes, state-of-the-art equipment, etc.

If a guy hit a two-hopper to shortstop in 1925, goes this rationale, he was thrown out at first by a step and a half. If a huge, finely-honed sprinter of the 1990s hits that same grounder to short — even on the hated fake grass — he's still going to be out by the same step and a half.

Baseball, they'll tell you, long ago achieved a delicate and almost mystical balance between pitcher and hitter, runner and fielder, offense and defense.

Oh yeah, and nobody from the horse-and-buggy days to this era of space shuttles and steroids *ever* hit a good high fastball.

Nobody.

You can look it up. Somewhere.

And what *was* Eckersley thinking, anyway?

Baseball's lore remains immutable. There's nothing even remotely like it in America's sports psyche.

However...

One thing even the most passionate defenders of the game cannot dispute is that baseball has suffered from a perception problem over, say, the past two decades.

The trouble stems from the fact that baseball does not translate well to television. Nor to that hustle-and-bustle, cell-phone mentality which seems to have gripped the populace as it speeds to who-knows-where.

TV thrives on fury, not relaxation. The medium simply cannot grasp nuance, or convey subtle strategems. Forget about outfielders moving a couple steps here or there, third-base coaches changing signs — and what about the smell of hot dogs?

So here we are at the turn of the century and baseball's newest acquaintances, potentially its next generation of fans, look at the game quite strangely. The way you'd view a distant landscape through out-of-focus binoculars, perhaps.

These people don't understand.

They've been glued to the tube or their little laptops so long that their eyeballs have glazed. They've lost the sensation of a summer evening entirely and, if they ever took a few minutes out of their hurly-burly schedules to watch a couple of innings, they'd promptly decide that baseball is far too tedious — or so terribly genteel that it belongs in a dusty museum.

In other words, hey, it's been 10 minutes and no one's torn an ACL. What, no concussions?

Click the remote and see if there's a crash on the NASCAR channel.

Clearly, the time has come to re-educate America about its game, to re-introduce baseball to its natural constituency.

It would be impossible, of course, to achieve such a thing in any kind of serious primer. Nobody'd read it.

The only solution is to address this audience on its own terms

— with humor, with irreverence, with cartoons.

And so, with all the humility of the game's true believers (none, in other words), we present: *101 Ways to Enjoy Baseball*.

We've kept this book relatively short, so you can hurry back to e-mailing someone in Pakistan or watching the WWF. And it's certainly been written simply, as though Einstein were beginning a lecture on the Theory of Relativity by pointing out the sky.

Best of all, this light-hearted treatise has been divided into three segments to reach each of baseball's novice audience groups: kids, women and potentially serious fans.

Yes, the final section may appeal primarily to men, but here's a warning, Mr. Hairy Chest: Don't skim it and try to sound like an expert, at least until you can recite "Casey at the Bat" from memory.

Don't even start it until you can explain the infield-fly rule.

OK, having set those provisos in place, we can approach the national pastime with the proper attitude. Which in baseball means simply: Have a good time.

And don't forget to stretch in the middle of the seventh inning.

BASEBALL FOR KIDS

This is where the game was meant to start.

In fact, baseball is a child's game which accidentally became popular enough to be played by adults. Later, for money. And eventually, for lots of money.

But it belongs to kids on a sandlot or playground.

Accordingly, our 101 ways to enjoy the game obviously should begin with the sprouts who will grow up playing it or someday sitting happily in the third-base box seats.

(Note: Since all baseball fans are young at heart, this section really is for everyone...)

No. 1

Play catch with your dad.

If he won't budge from the sofa, bang a tennis ball off the garage door until you get some action. It makes a lot of racket and leaves marks that Mom won't appreciate.

She'll get the old man outdoors, guaranteed.

No. 2

Try kickball at school.

That sounds silly, using your foot instead of a bat, but it's a good way to learn your way around the bases.

No. 3

Ask for the most expensive ball glove in the store for Christmas.

You won't get it, but your parents probably will throw in a bat and ball with that Joe Smutz model mitt.

No. 4

Play "Hot Box" every afternoon until it gets dark.

The older kids can show you how, mainly by making you be the one in the box most of the time.

That's okay, you'll grow up to be a good baserunner.

No. 5

Don't watch the guys on TV.

You'll wind up strutting around with four wristbands, two batting gloves and an earring instead of learning how to hit a fastball.

No. 6

Hey, Miss Jane, you can play, too.

Girls have just as much fun in chasing fly balls as boys do. You can join a Little League team, too. Tatum O'Neal threw a mean curveball in *The Bad News Bears*.

Just don't get so good that the guys won't let you into their games.

No. 7

Forget T-ball.

That's just a silly game invented by parents who want to sit around talking to each other while their toddlers walk around aimlessly.

Fly kites and chase butterflies until you're old enough to swing at a real pitch.

No. 8

Play Little League even if everybody else is better.

A lot of life's lessons have been learned standing alone in right field. Besides, getting that first uniform — the one that says "Moe's Pizza" — bonds you to baseball for life.

NO. 8

No. 9

Wear a cup.

Never mind what it is. Dad will show you.

No matter what age you are, eventually you'll get older and you're going to need some important parts.

No. 10

Want to see big boys play?

Drag your dad or brother to a high school game.

That's the best way to see serious hardball without spending a lot of money or accidentally learning to scratch yourself from crude professionals.

That'll come soon enough.

NO. 9

No. 11
Never cry.

No. 12
No, never.

Not even if that great big bully strikes you out four times and the catcher's going, "No batter, no batter!"

No crying in baseball — except when you're an adult and watch *Pride of the Yankees*.

No. 13

If there's a question of which league you should play in, don't listen to anybody else.

Your parents probably want to brag, and they'll stick you on a team with guys who shave.

There are three ways to know if you're ready for the next level:

1. Your uniform finally fits right.

2. You're hitting the ball hard enough that the third baseman yells, "Ow!"

3. You start noticing girls in the stands.

No. 14

Never laugh at other kids who aren't very good.

They may grow up to be skinny lefthanders with unhittable screwballs.

No. 15

Two rules of baseball: Bend your cap brim slightly and always keep the index finger outside your glove.

They're almost as important as not picking your nose while waiting for a relay throw.

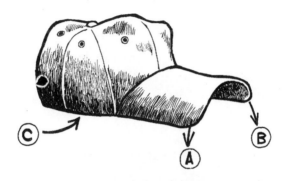

No. 16

Learn to slide in a big mud puddle.

You won't break anything — like your leg, for instance — and besides, you can have a super wrestling match afterwards.

No. 17

If your dad's a fan and wants to go see a pro game, be cool.

Don't start hollering for cotton candy every three pitches or you'll never get back.

Ask how to keep score. You won't understand it, but Pop will feel like Superman explaining things and he'll buy you a big ol' sundae on the way home.

No. 18

If your dad's a computer geek and won't go to a game, cut a deal.

Tell him if he drives you to a ballpark and pays for the seats, you'll promise to finish that science project that's stuck under your bed.

No. 19

Whenever you finally step inside a real ballpark, act like its Yankee Stadium.

Even minor leaguers in Twin Falls can turn a double play.

And you've got a better chance to catch a foul ball without 40,000 other kids trampling you to death.

No. 20

Ask for autographs.

Never mind why. It's a sacred obligation you'll understand when you're a dad.

No. 21

Whoever signs your scorebook, start checking the paper every day to see how he's doing.

Next summer, ask for the guy's uniform number on your own team.

No. 22

Keep your eye on the ball.

Doesn't matter where you are — playing second base, sitting in the bleachers, talking to your buddies way down the right-field line.

It is an absolute law of baseball, from 12-year-olds to the major leagues, that if you're daydreaming about fire engines or stock portfolios, you *will* get hit in the jaw.

No. 23

Do favors for your mom.

Maybe she'll wash and press your uniform — and especially your sanitaries, those long white things under your socks.

You play the way you look.

No. 24

If your parents try to talk you out of playing baseball, send for a copy of Mark McGwire's W-2.

Hint: He makes more money than Dad.

No. 25

As soon as your hands are big enough, learn to throw a knuckleball.

You might have a job for life.

BASEBALL FOR WOMEN

When you think about it, we may have reached a time when women are more likely to become baseball fans than men.

At least starting from scratch (no pun intended).

Guys are so busy buzzing around these days, gobbling power lunches and trying to fit in 20 minutes on the treadmill between business calls, they're probably not as inclined toward a timeless sport that can be as relaxing as Zen and takes even longer to master.

Women, on the other hand, enjoy breaks from the everyday madness.

They enjoy the ambience of a ballpark. And hey, what about all those guys in uniform who — unlike in most other sports — are neither 400-pound leviathans nor wrapped up head to toe in body armor?

Check out the stands at any minor- or major-league stadium. The gentler sex is startlingly well represented.

It only makes sense, then, to direct some cleverly crafted baseball nuggets toward the ladies.

Those of you who've already given up Tupperware parties to argue the merits of various middle relievers, uh, feel free to skip this section.

No. 26

Know something, anything, before you say a word.

The man in your life will roll his eyes if you ask why a foul ball isn't strike three.

No. 27

On the other hand, don't come off as an expert and expect Bubba to swoon.

If you know the next batter's lifetime average against the pitcher who's coming into the game and feel certain he's more likely to hit the ball on the ground than into the air...

Forget Bubba and go manage the White Sox.

NO. 26

No. 28

Dress the part.

Too many women show up at ballgames looking like they haven't changed clothes since Cannes. T-shirt, cut-offs and a ballcap, please.

Windbreaker for spring nights (all year in San Francisco and Oakland).

NO. 28

No. 29

No gawking.

Yes, some of the players are pretty darn cute, but most of 'em have wives sitting behind the dugout.

Start drooling over the third baseman and you'll not only miss a good game, you might be missing a boyfriend.

No. 30

Learn ballpark dating etiquette.

No matter if you're married, single, whatever. If you're watching a ballgame with somebody else, they want to see it, too.

"Honey, I'd love some peanuts and a Coke," is a reasonable request if made right at the end of an inning. With the bases loaded and two out, it's likely to be ignored outright.

No. 31

Ask any guy about his baseball career.

Chances are he didn't have one after high school, but men love to re-live dramatic moments of athletic heroism — even if they're embellished or totally fabricated.

An ex-jock recalling a two-run double he hit 20 years earlier is a very happy man.

No. 32

Don't critique the food.

Mr. Handsome sitting next to you doesn't want to hear about the nachos. He's totally absorbed watching the game — or maybe thinking how good you look in that halter top. Best not to interrupt either train of thought.

If you want to talk recipes or haute cuisine, invite him over or go to a restaurant.

No. 33
Check your allegiances.

Sometimes women who haven't become rabid fans feel like they have to cheer for one team, no matter what.

Nobody wants to hear you rooting for the bad guys just because you like their uniforms.

On the other hand, if you're really pledged, defend yourself.

Acceptable retort: "Whadda you care? My dad played for the Phillies, awright?"

No. 34
Don't take a book.

Divorces have started this way. If you're going to the game, at least pretend to be watching it.

You might be surprised.

No. 35

Don't make a fool of yourself at your own kid's game.

Cheer at the right times, be supportive, even keep quiet if necessary.

It could ruin your child's day — or his life — to hear you say, "You didn't pitch too badly. They only scored 11 runs."

The only thing worse than that is bellowing instructions, like: "C'mon, Billy, don't swing at pitches in the dirt."

After such a display, Billy will not ride home with you.

No. 36

Know the difference between a routine play and something spectacular.

Nobody wants to see a base hit shot cleanly up the middle and listen to you say, "How come nobody caught that?"

It was going 150 miles per hour, kiddo.

No. 37

Leave romance in the car.

Nobody, absolutely nobody at a ballgame wants to see a couple smooching in the bleachers.

They'll all be praying you both get beaned by a foul ball.

No. 38

Don't pack a lunch.

Most stadiums aren't going to allow coolers in the joint, anyway.

But even if they did, part of the baseball experience is ballpark food.

Junk? Sure, but great junk.

No. 39

Jeer when appropriate.

If the crowd turns on a particular player — or more likely, the umpire — feel free to call him any disgusting name that comes to mind.

It's no time to be ladylike when some bum can't throw strikes.

NO. 39

No. 40

Take your turn.

Buy a round. Offer to go get the next batch of dogs.

This ain't the prom.

No. 41

Thoughts of home?

Leave them at home.

It wrecks the whole day if you look wistfully toward center field and say, "Gee, that's beautiful grass. I wish we could get our lawn to look like that."

No. 42

Sense the mood.

When the good guys are up 8-1, Harry Hero has blasted a three-run homer and everyone around you is smiling, act like you've never been happier.

If Harry strikes out with two men on in the seventh, however, it's best to just sit around looking glum.

No. 43

Same as above, only change the scene to your kitchen table an hour after, say, a high school game.

Kids expect silent sympathy.

You won't win points by saying, "Sorry, honey, but I can't understand why you threw that big boy a curveball."

No. 44

He's a competitor, mom, not a fashion model. Never, never compliment your son on how he looks in his uniform. The kid might be clean and spiffy because he never got on base.

Dirty pants are a badge of honor in this game.

NO. 44

No. 45

Forget the Diamond Vision.

Real baseball fans care about the game, not the jingles, dot races, movie clips or whatever else teams put up on the screen just to make noise. If you want to see *Titanic,* rent it on the way home.

No. 46

Don't holler on every pitch.

This isn't football, where sustained insanity goes with the territory.

Baseball has its moments of great excitement and high drama, but it's up to you to know when they occur.

Going ballistic over a foul tip will blow your cover.

No. 47

Nobody wants to see a Mary Poppins, either.

Coming off like little Miss Prim, clapping politely like you're watching a Broadway musical, is every bit as irritating as acting like a nut case.

Learn the game and don't be afraid to cheer.

No. 48

Don't ask about the black stuff under the players' eyes.

Every novice does, and every savvy fan cringes when he hears it.

It's to dull the glare on bright afternoons, by the way, which may cause you to ask why everyone isn't wearing sunglasses. Batters need to see the spin on the ball, that's why.

No. 49

Even if your husband or boyfriend hates baseball, you can still be a fan.

Respond this way: "Hey, you wouldn't care if I joined a book club in my free time. So what's wrong with cheering for the Mets?"

He doesn't have any answer that won't make him sound like a jealous goof, so you win.

Go enjoy yourself.

No. 50

They're fun to watch play, but don't marry one.

Pretend you're having a great time at the races. Would you want a thoroughbred grazing in your backyard?

BASEBALL FOR THE EXPERT

So you want to be a seamhead?

That's journalist jargon for anyone who becomes consumed by baseball. For instance, committing the won-lost records of the entire Texas Rangers pitching staff to memory but forgetting your children's birthdays.

Seamhead isn't necessarily meant as a derogatory term, although incessant yammering about earned run averages and sprewing out streams of stats from the Mexican League might put something of a goofball spin on the term.

Actually, there are some very serious people studying baseball.

Universities offer courses in various disciplines associated with the game.

That might be taking things a bit beyond the norm, but hey, this sport has inspired plenty of lifetime afflictions.

Certainly baseball, once you get beneath the surface, is the most complicated major sport.

"Every time you think you understand it, this game will jump up and bite you on the butt," former major league coach and manager Rene Lachmann once announced.

Heck, a respected author wrote a huge, hard-cover book which covered the events in *one* game between the Orioles and Brewers.

Yeah, that might be a bit much, but...

Pay attention and decide for yourself.

No. 51

Start with the basics.

For instance, how many players to a side?

Nine, you say? Not so fast.

The correct answer: "Depends which league you're talking about.

There are 10 players if a designated hitter is involved."

No. 52

Enlist expert help.

Living next door to someone like Sparky Anderson would be an advantage, but you might have to settle for Joe at the office — the guy who wrote his doctoral thesis on the pros and cons of the squeeze play.

No. 53

Never join a rotisserie league.

Avoid people who do.

The lowest form of baseball life is a stat freak who doesn't know grass from dirt in the real world.

No one is more boring than a guy who can give you the on-base percentage of every player on the 1925 Yankees but doesn't know who should cover second on a comebacker to the mound.

No. 54

Square this new passion with your significant other.

Concessions might be necessary if you're going to lie awake, thrashing and muttering that Manny Muscles never should have swung at that 3-and-0 pitch.

Worst case scenario: Agree to attend an opera.

No. 55

Go find a couple of authentic baseball movies, like *Bull Durham*.

Do not, however, view them with children present.

Likewise, get a feel for the ambience of the game without picking up the bad language.

No. 56

Find an authentic Louisville Slugger bat, cover the handle with pine tar and heft it whenever the spirit strikes — all the better to "touch" the game.

Beware of lampshades and expensive Ming vases, however.

No. 57

Use a V-chip or whatever other device is necessary to block ESPN from all your TVs.

SportsCenter's non-stop clips of monstrous home runs makes the game look like slow-pitch softball and has ruined more young players than the aluminum bat.

No. 58

Learn to keep score.

You wouldn't want to live in a foreign country without knowing the language, would you?

Everyone's scorebook scribbles are slightly different, but the basic symbols remain — and you'll never grasp the game until you can instantly picture a 3-6-3 double play.

No. 59

Absorb this passion slowly.

Baseball is a game of pace, pitch to pitch, inning to inning, season to season.

It doesn't fit the hurry-up world, and if you try learning too much, too fast, you'll end up embarrassing yourself at the water cooler.

"Barry Blowhard was throwing it 98 miles an hour last night," you say to impress the guys.

"Fast gun or slow gun?" somebody asks.

You're out on strikes.

No. 60
Slowly, Part II

Bad form is taking your 12-year-old to a ballgame and screaming, "He dropped it!"

Only to have the kid yawn and say, "That was the shortstop, Dad. They already called the infield-fly rule. Duh..."

No. 61

If you begin to wax eloquent about your new love of baseball and a neighbor says he played some ball, nod and talk about pruning the roses.

Everyone, absolutely everyone, is tempted to respond, "Me, too."

Resist the impulse. It always ends in disaster.

No. 62

Sit comfortably late some night and quietly hold a baseball.

Stay silent.

Knowledge will flow from mystical sources, and you will feel one with the game.

For obvious reasons, avoid being observed.

No. 63

Commit to memory this everlasting truth: The truest test of a great hitter is his ability to get the run home with a man on third and less than two out.

NO. 60

No. 64

State flatly that Pete Rose *should* be in the Hall of Fame.

No. 65

Announce at every opportunity: "Bo Jackson was the worst baseball player of his generation."

No. 66

Do not attempt to explain any of those three aforementioned bedrocks of baseball faith.

It's way, way too soon.

Your early exercises are analogous to learning the names of the planets before applying to fly the space shuttle.

Remember, baseball cannot be rushed.

No. 67

Okay, okay, since curiosity is killing you, here's the primer version of the three great truths:

1. You win by scoring, and lose by blowing easy scoring opportunities. Case closed.

2. Enshrinement in the Hall is for baseball accomplishment only. Heck, Ty Cobb shot somebody and was elected nearly unanimously.

3. Bo had the worst clutch-hitting statistics of any player in a similar time period, never threw the ball to the right base and struck out more times in his first four seasons than Joe DiMaggio did in an entire career.

No. 68

Go to a game and just shut up.

Don't holler at the umps, don't scream for the beer man, don't bellow for a new pitcher.

And don't use binoculars.

Just take it in — sights, sounds and smells.

No. 69

Spend one entire summer learning the difference between a two-seam and four-seam fastball.

They have as much in common as ice cream and caviar.

No. 70

As you begin to pick up baseball jargon, take care that you're up to date.

Don't say "dinger" for a home run. The current reference is "big fly."

Fastballs used to be "gas." At the moment (but subject to immediate change), a good hard one is "cheese."

NO. 70

No. 71

Go ahead and watch a game on TV, but pay attention ONLY to camera shots from center field.

Your mission is to study the relationship between pitcher and catcher.

This is the essence of baseball.

Besides, as Pittsburgh Pirate lefty Bob Veale once observed: "Good pitching always beats good hitting, and vice versa."

NO. 71

No. 72

Appreciate the peanut.

No matter what your political affiliation and/or feelings for noted peanut farmer Jimmy Carter, this is the shelled jewel of baseball.

If you leave a ballpark without consuming at least three bags of peanuts, you may be subject to unexpected anxiety, migraine headaches and frightening memory loss.

As in: Who hit that double in the seventh inning?

NO. 72

No. 73

Loathe all mascots.

They belong in a circus, not on the holy greensward.

No. 74

Learn to spit.

It'll bond you emotionally to the athletes.

NO. 73

No. 75

Now, work on spitting regularly and with sincere emotion — excitement, disgust, boredom, whatever.

You actually might be mistaken for a major-league manager and asked for your autograph.

No. 76

Create a test to gauge your progress as a student of the game.

For instance, write a 1,000-word essay on why every team needs two lefties in the bullpen.

NO. 75

No. 77

Experiment with the real thing.

Seek out a professional pitcher and ask him to throw 10 or 12 pitches while you stand in the batter's box.

At least one pitch should be a curveball that buzzes straight for your coconut but snaps across the plate for a strike.

Do not feel less of a person if you wet your pants.

No. 78

Imagine that you are a newspaper reporter.

What questions would you ask the manager about that ninth-inning decision that went wrong?

And how would you respond after he calls you a moron?

No. 79

Imagine that you are a TV reporter.

On second thought, don't. You'll spend too much time worrying about your hair.

NO. 78

No. 80

Learn to decipher this phrase: "I was just trying to stay within myself."

No. 81

See if you can steal a sign from any big-league third base coach.

Announcing aloud that the hit-and-run is on marks you as a promising seamhead.

Assuming that you're right, of course.

If the batter takes the pitch and the runner stays put, you may want to spend the next couple of innings in the men's room.

No. 82

Never state the obvious.

For instance, nudging your buddy and telling him that a hitter is looking for a fastball on a 3-and-1 count is strictly bush league stuff.

Every batter in every league in every solar system is looking for a fastball on 3-and-1.

No. 83

Study the box scores in your morning newspaper.

No, not for fantasy league numbers.

Any advanced seamhead can re-create an entire game — including scratches, twitches and jock-strap adjustments — by scanning the box score.

No. 84

Never argue about stats.

Boring.

If someone persists in vomiting up Rickey Henderson's strike-out-to-walk ratio in day games versus night games, ask him if can name 10 ways for a pitcher to commit a balk.

No. 85

Whenever you're at the park, see if you can out-guess the official scorer on whether a batted ball should be ruled a hit or an error.

This is totally subjective. The scorer doesn't know, either.

What matters is that you have a reason for your call and can explain it for five full minutes without pausing for breath.

No. 86

Avoid Dodger fans unless they can trace their roots all the way back to Brooklyn.

Why would you listen to quiche-eaters from Los Angeles who leave games in the seventh inning?

NO. 86

No. 87

Never try to sound smart by calling for a bunt.

Percentage wise, it's the worst play in baseball.

Yep. Look it up.

No. 88

Throw away those mystery novels for airplane reading and jump into the *Official Rules of Baseball*.

Nothing passes the time on a five-hour flight like parsing out every nuance of catcher's interference.

No. 89

Never, never stare at an attractive woman.

Not at the ballpark, anyway.

What if the shortstop moves three steps to his left while your attention is diverted?

No. 90

Have the courage to say aloud that *Fields of Dreams* was no real baseball movie.

And even worse, that it depicted Shoeless Joe batting from the wrong side of the plate.

No. 91

Don't bother to reach for foul balls hit into the stands.

Kid's stuff.

You're supposed to be thinking about what kind of pitch was fouled off, why, and how it might change pitch selection for the rest of the at-bat.

No. 92

Liven up parties by demonstrating both legal and illegal take-out slides on potential double plays.

Avoid the punch bowl.

No. 93

Everyone knows which ballparks have natural grass and which are cursed with artificial turf.

You should know the brand names or seed types.

Celestial seamheads know which direction the grass has been mowed and whether or not it might affect a ball bouncing into the gap.

No. 94

Be able to take a blind taste test and identify hot dogs from every venue in the Gulf Coast League.

Bonus points for correctly determining actual cooking time.

NO. 94

No. 95

Learn the exact medical definition — and recovery time — for every common baseball injury.

Drop the word "subluxation" into cocktail party conversations.

Note: There are several living seamheads who claim to have performed the "Tommy John operation" on themselves.

No. 96

Keep a divorce lawyer's business card in your wallet at all times.

No. 97

As your passion evolves from enthusiasm to cult-like, spare your children.

Your 8-year-old who wants to play catch does NOT need to throw Kevin Brown's sinker.

No. 98

Keep your knowledge pure.

Avoid the All-Star game.

No. 99

Never gloat.

Having correctly predicted the exact pitch on which a hitter would pop the ball to very short right, and that the runner would score from third anyway because the outfielder has been bothered by tendinitis, you need not say another word.

Even a great game can be ruined by a punch in the nose.

No. 100

Begin looking for some new friends.

Your old pals won't speak the lingo and you'll be boring them stiff.

Start searching for a seamhead chat room on the Internet, and debate arcane questions until the wee hours.

NO. 99

No. 101

Find a job in baseball.

You're bound to lose your present one.

NO. 101

THE AUTHOR

Steve Cameron, a crafty lefthander who couldn't throw hard enough to make a living at it, has been a reporter, columnist and author for nearly 30 years. He has covered baseball at every level from the California League to the World Series.

The author of 10 books, including best-selling biographies of Brett Favre and George Brett, Cameron currently is sports editor of *The Daily Herald*, a newspaper serving the area south of Salt Lake City.

Cameron lives with his wife, Sylvia, and Margaret (14), Michael (12) and Miss Jane (10) in Pleasant Grove, Utah.

Other Addax Sports-Humor Books

It's 3rd and Long, So ... 101 Ways to Improve the Game of Football
By Clay Latimer

This humorous book proposes 101 ways to improve football. Some are cynical, some fanciful, some radical - and none has a shot at being enacted until Tampa Bay freezes over. Hard cover, 144 pages. Retail Price $9.95.

Mulligans 4 All! 101 Excuses, Alibis and Observation on the Game of Golf
By Chuck Carson

Mulligans 4 All! offers 101 ways to make golf fun, fulfilling, interesting and may even cut down on your use of the words you don't want your children saying. Hilarious cartoons highlight the action. Hard cover, 144 pages. Retail price $9.95.

To order individual or bulk copies of
these books please contact.
Addax Publishing Group, Inc.
8643 Hauser Drive, Suite 235
Lenexa, KS 66215
1-800-598-5550